D1579539

The National Galleries of Scotland, in its three buildings, the Portrait Gallery, the National Gallery and the Gallery of Modern Art, holds the nation's collection of Scottish art. It is a marvellously rich and varied collection ranging in date from the 16th century to the present day, including works by artists of world stature and by others hardly known outside the Galleries themselves.

SCOTTISH MASTERS is a new series designed to make some of the most interesting and delightful Scottish artists more widely known. In 1984 the Patrons of the National Galleries of Scotland was founded under the Presidency of HRH The Duke of Edinburgh to channel extra financial assistance from the private sector to the National Galleries. They are enormously grateful to the Scottish Post Office Board for the generous sponsorship of this series. This has enabled these attractively designed monographs to be published at such a reasonable price. How appropriate that the masters of communications themselves should help us to communicate to Scotland, and beyond, the heritage of us all.

Explanation is an essential part of the Galleries' purpose: so also is acquisition. We are doubly grateful to the Scottish Post Office Board for the generous financial help they have given us to boost our active policy of purchasing the finest works of Scottish art for our national collections. We are delighted that the Board share our view that for a lively gallery acquisition and explanation must go hand in hand.

The Scottish Post Office Board's imaginative support of the National Galleries is just one part of their enlightened programme of involvement with both visual and performing arts, reminding us of the central role that the Post Office plays in Scottish life.

THE VISCOUNT WEIR,
Chairman of the Patrons of the National Galleries of Scotland.

ANGUS GROSSART,
Chairman of the Trustees of the National Galleries of Scotland.

John Zephaniah Bell (1794–1883)
Self-portrait
Oil on canvas   38 × 32 cm (sight)
(Private collection)

John Zephaniah

BELL

1794–1883

BY HELEN SMAILES

JOHN ZEPHANIAH BELL

'Who J. Z. Bell is we know not – oh, a Scot, if we may judge from the Catalogue, "Canongate, Edinburgh". His *Lady Jane Grey refusing the crown* is very clever. The shadows – but we must not mind trifles – the conception is original and peculiar.' The supercilious reviewer in the *Gentleman's Magazine* of 1832 could not have realised the full import of his remarks. He had just awarded Bell one of the few critical accolades of a productive career spanning fifty years of the nineteenth century. He had also anticipated Bell's ultimate decline into obscurity, his death unnoticed even by the Royal Scottish Academy of which he was one of the earliest members.

By 1832 Bell had made his mark as a distinctive portraitist owing little to any Scottish predecessor. He was the friend and assistant of Sir David Wilkie. With a proven aptitude for decorative painting Bell had mastered the art of fresco ten years before the public competitions for the decoration of the Palace of Westminster. At the same time he showed a penchant for literary genre and history painting. This versatility was to contribute to his failure to achieve critical recognition or sustained patronage in any one genre. Then, in 1843, he sabotaged a promising career as an educator by remaining on the wrong side of the doctrinal conflict at the Manchester School of Design. His final decision to settle in London was to prove a passport to obscurity. A century later the problems of the modern art historian have been compounded by the dispersal of most of his pictures and the total lack of contemporary documentation in the form of family correspondence, journals or sitters' books.

It is to an article in the *Manchester City News* that we owe the only consecutive account of Bell's early life and his develop-ment during the 1820s and 1830s when he produced his most original work.[1] He was born in Dundee in 1794, the second son among the sixteen children of William Bell and Anna Young. William Bell was a substan-tial figure in the Dundee business community with a controlling interest in a local tannery and sugar refinery, in shipping companies in Dundee, Montrose, Aberdeen and Leith, and in the Dundee New Bank. His fortunes deteriorated irreversibly when, in 1799, he was persuaded by his elder brother James to move to London in order to salvage the affairs of two subsidiary family businesses. Ruined and embittered by financial mismanagement, William returned to Scotland in 1806 and was drawn into sequestration proceedings which were still in progress at the time of his death in 1834.[2]

In Edinburgh John Zephaniah received a sound classical education at the Royal High School under Alexander Adam. While training for the law, he was advised by an unnamed miniature painter to take up art. In 1817, armed with an introduction to Wilkie, Bell enrolled at the Royal Academy Schools where he studied painting under the portraitist Martin Archer Shee.[3] Unlike Wilkie, Bell did not seek admission to the Trustees' Academy in Edinburgh before gravitating to London. The deciding factor was probably the absence of any provision for life drawing for which no institutionalised facilities existed in Edinburgh until 1829 when the Royal Institution opened a Life Class. It seems likely that it was during Bell's studentship at the Academy that he learned that Wilkie, 'finding much difficulty to meet the demand for his works, got assistance towards their execution from Fraser [i.e. Alexander Fraser, the genre painter], who carried them on so far from Wilkie's sketches and directions. Mr. Bell proposed the same to Sir David, who immediately closed with it, and put into his hands a deal of work; and when Mr. Bell's other occupations stopped this, told him that he should always be glad of his help.' At all events, Bell did not stay the

(ten–year) course at the Academy Schools. Disenchanted with the teaching of drawing, he sought admission to the Parisian studio of David's most distinguished pupil, Antoine Gros.

For a Scottish artist of his generation, Bell's initiative was not merely unorthodox, but probably unprecedented. Gros's atelier in the Institut de France was effectively a private academy whose reputation exceeded that of the Ecole des Beaux-Arts itself. Gros's advocacy of draughtsmanship as the first principle of art education and the high priority accorded to life drawing and to close individual supervision were derived from the practice of David.[4] The appearance of the atelier was recorded in a fascinating painting by Auguste Massé, a pupil of Baron Gros in

Fig 1
GROS'S STUDIO IN PARIS
by Auguste Antoine Massé
(Musée Marmottan, Paris)

1818 (fig 1). Bell himself followed an intensive regime, also copying in the Louvre and devoting his evenings to further life drawing at the Académie Suisse, run by the former model 'le père Suisse'.

In Paris Bell formed one of the most influential associations of his early career. From 1820 David Ogilvy, later 9th Earl of Airlie, lived in Paris, returning to Scotland only when his title was confirmed by Act of Parliament in 1826. Bell's relationship with the Airlies appears to have been as cordial as differences in social status would allow. Through the Airlies he gained an introduction to David Bailie Warden, the former American consul and a member of the French Academy, and thereby an entrée into the highest social circles frequented by Baron Vivant Denon, Napoleon's director-general of museums.

In 1825 Bell took a second decision of vital importance. His journey to Rome via Lyons and the Rhone valley was undertaken partly on foot in order to avail himself of every opportunity for sketching. He was to remain in Italy, principally in Rome, for fifteen months. On his own Continental tour in 1826 Wilkie noted that, 'the Italians and French are alike followers of David; the English students . . . are chiefly occupied with subjects of Roman costume; while the Germans . . . have revived the art of fresco.' In May 1826 Bell wrote to the Countess of Airlie that he had made his 'maiden attempt at Historical Painting' and that Wilkie shared his fascination with the picturesque costumes of Italy.[5] Most significantly, as recorded by the *Manchester City News,* he was studying the frescoes of Cimabue and Giotto and associating with 'the German artists who then devoted themselves

to that manner of working – Schnorr and Gegenbaur. The latter most courteously taught him to paint in fresco, inviting him to work in his room beside him.' Julius Schnorr von Carolsfeld was one of the principal members of the artist brotherhood whose preoccupations and piety had earned them the title of the 'Nazarenes'. The Nazarene community had acquired a mesmeric attraction for artists and connoisseurs passing through Rome. Their revolutionary proposal for the revival of large-scale fresco painting as the instrument of national artistic regeneration was to fuel an entire movement for State patronage of fresco in Britain. By 1825 the Nazarenes had completed the decoration of the Casa Bartholdy and were similarly engaged at the Casino Massimo where Schnorr's contributions were especially admired. Such was their impact that Wilkie's correspondence for 1825–6 is filled with references to their experiment and the desirability of emulating it in Britain. Bell's second tutor in fresco, Anton von Gegenbaur (an associate rather than a member of the Nazarene inner circle), was to offer similar instruction to David Scott in 1833.[6]

The cumulative experience of Paris and Italy gave Bell the competence and the incentive to submit works to the main exhibiting bodies in Britain. In 1824–5 he made his debut at the Academy, the British Institution, the Royal Society of British Artists and the Northern Society for the Encouragement of the Fine Arts in Leeds. From 1828 he also contributed to the annual exhibitions of the Academy of Liverpool Royal Institution. His Liverpool intermediary was the painter and collector, Nathaniel George Philips, with whom he had formed a close friendship during sketching excursions in the Roman Campagna.

In letters written between 1827 and Philip's premature death in August 1831 Bell confided at length his personal and artistic concerns. In 1828 he was elected an Associate of the Institution for the Encouragement of the Fine Arts in Scotland. The next year he was among twenty-four Scottish artists of recognised standing who petitioned successfully for admission to the rival institution, the Scottish Academy. As an Associate of the Institution, Bell was granted the full status of Academician.[7] Official honours scarcely compensated for his desperation that he had not 'made a rap' by his profession since returning to Edinburgh. On at least one occasion Philips sold some of his own stock of pictures to relieve his friend's penury.

Bell's frustration was intensified by his own self-assurance. As a portraitist he was reduced to appealing to Philips for introductions to 'some of your Liverpool Merchants who may wish themselves taken off; for here the Edinburgers are . . . so satisfied with John Watson (later Watson Gordon) being the Vandyck of Scotland that they will look no farther.' Ironically, it was in this capacity that Bell produced his most distinguished surviving work (plate 6). The double portrait of the Earl of Airlie and his daughter was shown at the Institution in 1829 together with a second portrait of the Earl. In the rigorous integration of its design, combined with subtle and even sensuous exploration of rich textures, the picture reveals the extent of Bell's indebtedness to the portraiture of David. The slightly disquieting intensity of the relationship between the two figures and their dramatic engagement with the artist was to remain a hallmark of his finest portraits (see plate 8). Equally characteristic is his delight in romantic landscape as a secondary subject in its own right rather than as an inherited convention of formal portraiture.

The second reason for Bell's plight was his dominant perception of himself and that of his potential patrons as 'the star of the grand style' so that, 'they think it a pity to occupy my precious pencil with their tame mugs and to pay *any* price for my inspired compositions.' As an aspiring history painter he relied on Philips for vital personal encouragement, exhibiting opportunities which might solicit public patronage, and the occasional private purchase. In 1828 Philips released for exhibition and possible sale at the Liverpool Academy *The Shunamite lady coming to Elisha after the death of her son.* Two years later Bell was engrossed in a large picture (measuring over seven feet by five feet) of *Lady Jane Grey refusing the crown,* composed with fastidious attention to historical costume and architectural detail.[8] In the same genre he was developing into a 'prodigious colourist' and in 1828 he described his diploma picture for the Institution, *Jephthah meeting his daughter,* as 'strong and bright as Titian'.

In addition to experimenting with landscape in watercolour on the recommendation of Wilkie, Bell was exploring fresco as an adjunct to history painting. In 1827 he discussed with Philips a cartoon of *Job and his comforters* for exhibition at Somerset House and in July 1831 he was forced by recurrent attacks of severe pain (probably migraine) to jettison a fresco destined for the Liverpool Academy. The following month, in a personal letter to the Earl of Airlie, he announced his marriage to the eldest daughter of Charles Campbell, the head of an Argyllshire family who had settled in Edinburgh. Jane Graham Hay Campbell, some thirteen years his junior, had sat to the artist 'for love' for a portrait exhibited at the Institution in 1829. The Campbells had 'good connections, but still, rather high notions . . . and not more money, than enables them to keep up a genteel appearance.' The marriage was strongly opposed by Jane's parents who were doubtless aware of the precariousness of Bell's professional circumstances. Faced with the prospect of an elopement, Campbell agreed to a private ceremony at his own house. The marriage, which took place on 31 August, was to produce a family of six children of whom the eldest daughter, Jane Campbell Bell, exhibited at the Academy between 1850 and 1863.[9]

In the same letter Bell referred to his current project for the Earl which promised to open up a 'capital prospect', both financial and artistic. His studio was then occupied by the cartoon for a fresco destined for Cortachy Castle near Kirriemuir, where the ceiling and walls of the dining room were to be decorated with narrative paintings celebrating the achievements of the Earl's ancestors.[10] This pioneering scheme was subsequently de-stroyed, perhaps during the extensive remod-elling of Cortachy by David Bryce. The attendant social prestige attracted a second major commission at a time when public patronage for fresco painting in Britain did not extend beyond theoretical debate and private patronage was virtually unheard of.[11]

Shortly after Bell's engagement, 'two gentlemen called on me, and after seeing the cartoon for your fresco, entered into negotia-tions about painting and designing ceilings;

and since that, I have heard of a third. Besides all this, when I was in London, three painters of first rate eminence advised me to come up there, for that a good field lay before me.' Among these prospective clients was Captain William Davidson who, after spending many years abroad, was building a Tudor-Gothic mansion on his estate of Muirhouse at Granton near Edinburgh. Davidson's lavish expenditure was to prove such a drain on his finances that he staged a suicide by drowning in 1834.[12] Although a professional soldier, Davidson 'displayed superior taste in matters of art' and his son Thomas later studied painting under Delaroche and Vernet, perhaps as a result of Bell's influence.

As late as 1883 the two frescoes executed by Bell in 1832 in the public rooms of Muirhouse were still visible and in pristine condition – a measure of his rare competence to which William Dyce testified in 1841.[13] The sole surviving ceiling fresco (cover), is painted in trompe l'oeil perspective with consummate mastery of foreshortening and characteristic sensitivity in the handling of drapery. (The differentiation in texture in the man's doublet is rendered by deep incisions into the wet plaster.) In composition the fresco is clearly related to a genre study modelled by the artist's two sisters (plate 5) and exhibited at the Royal Academy in 1832. Stylistically the Muirhouse ceiling suggests an affinity with the Nazarenes and Bell's probable familiarity with the paintings of Piazzetta and Tiepolo. Wilkie was in no doubt as to the importance of Bell's achievement. On 21 November 1833 he drafted a letter of introduction to the sculptor Sir Francis Chantrey, recommending Bell as 'the reviver of painting in Fresco in Scotland' and in August 1834 he paid a special visit to Muirhouse in company with John Lister. Wilkie's admiration was shared by 'Scotus' of Edinburgh who, in June 1833, wrote to *The Times* to assert the prior claims of Bell as the promoter of a fresco revival in Britain.

Buoyed up by the reception of his two Scottish commissions, Bell exhibited the cartoons for his Muirhouse project at the Academy in 1835. Concurrently he showed a sketch for a narrative picture of Richard II 'intended to have been painted in fresco on an arched panel 28 feet long in the grand staircase of the new Goldsmiths' Hall' (see page 14). Bell's abortive bid for metropolitan patronage was surely timed to coincide with the publication by the Select Committee on the Arts and Manufactures of a report including the first official proposal for State support for fresco. However, in 1841, his former teacher Shee recorded in evidence before the Select Committee the continued frustration of Bell's ambitions as a decorative painter: 'On inquiring recently, as to the success of his enterprise, I learned from him that he had given it up, for he found he had no chance in competition with the upholsterer.'[14]

In the autumn of 1833 Bell achieved the curious distinction of becoming the only British artist to paint the fourteen-year-old Dona Maria da Glória (later Maria II) during the siege of Lisbon in the concluding phase of the Portuguese civil war. The full-length portrait now graces a function room named after Dona Maria in the town hall of Portugal's second city Oporto. It is signed and dated 'Lisbon October 1833' (plate 7). The picture is undocumented apart from a tradition alleging a civic commission. Its

precise status is as debatable as the motivation of the artist's extraordinary journey to Portugal.

The civil war of 1832–4 is as much a forgotten episode of British foreign policy as an integral part of the history of Portugal and the general context of Bell's picture must be the proliferation of British military involvement in Portugal during the Peninsular Wars. By this date British (and, more specifically, Scottish) merchants dominated the port wine export trade centred on Oporto. The Factory House built in the Rua Nova dos Ingleses by the British consul during the 1790s as the social and trading centre of the expatriate community (fig 2) was clearly conceived as a national rather than a purely localised symbol of British mercantile influence in Portugal.[15]

In 1826 Pedro I of Brazil and IV of Portugal drew up a constitutional charter on the British parliamentary model. He then abdicated the Portuguese throne in favour of his younger daughter Dona Maria on condition that she eventually marry his brother

Fig 2
THE BRITISH FACTORY HOUSE, OPORTO
Engraving from J. C. Murphy,
Travels in Portugal, *1795*

Fig 3
OPORTO FROM THE QUAY OF VILA NOVA DA GAIA
Illustration from Lt. Col. R. Batty, Select Views of Some of the Principal Cities of Europe, *1832*

Dom Miguel. As Regent, Miguel repudiated the charter and declared himself absolute monarch, driving his niece and the constitutionalist party into exile. In 1831 Dom Pedro resigned his Brazilian throne to head the struggle against his brother on behalf of Dona Maria. Calling first at London, he negotiated a substantial loan and essential British military support. In July 1832 he reached Oporto (fig 3), the centre of liberal resistance to the Miguelite regime.[16]

Apart from regular British troops Dom Pedro was recruiting mercenaries by means of an Anglo-Portuguese Commission operating from London. In the autumn of 1833 alluring advertisements appeared in Scottish newspapers, offering generous remuneration and allocations of land in Portugal on the conclu-sion of hostilities. The Reform agitators, unfortunates and undesirables of Edinburgh and Glasgow who sailed from the Clyde mostly joined Dom Pedro's crack regiment of foreigners, the Fusileiros Escocêses, commanded by their fellow-countryman, Colonel Charles Shaw.[17] One of these Scottish troop ships almost certainly carried Bell to Lisbon. In September his younger brother James Stanislaus, a Glasgow merchant burgess, was appointed Portuguese vice-consul for Glasgow and the Clyde ports with jurisdiction over all Scottish trade to Portugal. In addition he was employed as a regional recruiting agent and was soon receiving bitter complaints from the unpaid, undernourished and mutinous Fusileiros who had failed to found a new Glasgow.[18]

On 10 and 11 October the Miguelite forces were finally repulsed from Lisbon during a fierce engagement led by Dom Pedro. This sequence of events bears out the anecdote about the painting of Queen Maria's portrait during the siege, as recorded by the *Manchester City News*. The setting was the small Palácio da Necessidades, delightfully situated on a hill on the western outskirts of Lisbon with panoramic views of the Tagus. Mindful of the impoverished state of Portugal, the royal family had moved there for the sake of economy. On finishing the portrait Bell spent a day observing the battle at close quarters, later recounting his impressions to Wilkie.

Owing to the hazards of cross–country travel, it is unlikely that Bell ever reached Oporto. According to family tradition he narrowly escaped suffocation under a collapsible bed canopy while staying at an inn in hostile (Miguelite) territory! He must have left Portugal soon after the raising of the siege of Lisbon for by November he was back in London. At the Academy in 1834 the portrait was ignored by reviewers – an unaccountable omission given its quality, size and topicality. (Dona Maria became Queen in September 1834.) In 1835 Bell commissioned a mezzotint from the London engraver William Ward, embellished with a humble dedication in Portuguese to the Queen's stepmother, the Duchess of Bragança.[19]

Following his bankruptcy in Glasgow in 1835 James Stanislaus Bell was himself drawn into a minor international incident. In association with a third Bell brother he embarked on a rash speculation in salt on the coast of Circassia in the northern Caucasus. In 1836 the enterprise came to grief when their

Fig 4
FRONTISPIECE BY J. S. BELL
for his Circassian Journal, *published 1840*

ship the *Vixen* was seized by the Russians who claimed sovereignty over the territory. Retrieving what he could from the disaster, James published in 1840 a travelogue illustrated with his own sketches (fig 4). Circassian pictures, a specialist variant of romantic orientalism, owed much of their popularity to Sir William Allan. In 1841 John Zephaniah showed at the Academy *Circassians reconnoitring a Russian position*. The picture was presumably based on his brother's sketches and was accompanied by a catalogue reference to his Circassian journal.[20]

By the late 1830s, with a wife and young family to support, Bell was still struggling with financial hardship. In 1837 Wilkie secured for his protégé the Mastership of the new Manchester School of Design.[21] The School owed its origins to a growing conviction among British manufacturers that it was imperative to improve national standards of design, as a matter both of principle and of commercial expediency in response to European competition. This awareness crystallised in the report of the Select Committee on the Arts and Manufactures in 1835. In 1837 the government-sponsored Central School of Design opened in London and in 1838 William Dyce was appointed Director. From 1841 funds were released for auxiliary schools in major provincial cities. In the meantime Benjamin Robert Haydon, having deplored the state of art education in Manchester, activated the local manufacturers.[22] Their School opened in October 1838 in the Mosley Street premises of the Manchester Institution (fig 5).

Fig 5
MANCHESTER ROYAL INSTITUTION
*Site of the School of Design
and now the City Art Gallery*

An invaluable history of the School was written by Bell's pupil Robert Crozier. At first the School was virtually autonomous, being supported by the subscriptions of Mancunian manufacturers and the students' fees. As Master, Bell answered to the local management committee rather than the authorities of the London School. The manufacturers' motivation was basically, but not exclusively, utilitarian: they anticipated annual savings of some £20,000 on the cost of importing French designs for calico printing. The prototype for their academy was the School of Design at Lyons. In his 1838 report to the Board of Trade on continental art education Dyce singled out the Lyons School as the only French institution with a proven record of improving design in (silk) manufacture. His reservations focused on the universal priority given to life study and the related fact that all students, including artisans, 'commence as if they intended to become artists in the higher sense of the word'. In contrast Dyce advocated a studio-workshop system which would guarantee vocational training appropriate to the artisan and preserve him from aspiring to mediocrity as a fine artist. Both Bell and Dyce were to cite the example of Lyons in support of their divergent theoretical positions.[23]

From the outset Bell adopted a modified equivalent of the French atelier system. The doctrinal dispute which was to rend the School began when its original patrons applied for a government subsidy to match private funding. The application was granted – Manchester ranked as a high priority – on condition that the curriculum be revised in conformity with the practice of the Central School. In January 1843 an unequivocal policy statement, drafted by Dyce, was forwarded to the Manchester committee. Henceforth facilities for life drawing were to be severely curtailed. For some months Bell held out with the majority support of the manufacturers. Finally, undermined by internal factionalism, he resigned. When the life class was suspended, a group of his former students formed a secessionist society for life drawing known as the 'Roman Bricks'. Their society continued to meet for twenty-two years, the qualification for admission being training under J. Z. Bell.[24]

Ironically, Bell seems to have supported the principle of the institution of the Schools of Design. He took issue with their methodology. In 1846, having settled in London, he set up a private academy at his house in Upper Charlotte Street, Fitzroy Square, offering a continental style of tuition. In November *The Spectator* devoted a feature to Bell's academy as the most important new educational facility for the arts of design in London and the potential counterpart to the celebrated ateliers of Vernet and Delaroche.[25]

Bell was drawn to London by the prospect of a revitalised career as a history painter subsidised by the State. At the Manchester Institution he drew two large cartoons, *Cardinal Bourchier* and *Samson Agonistes,* for the first Westminster competition of 1843. In 1841 a Select Committee was formed to debate the promotion of the fine arts in relation to the reconstruction of the Houses of Parliament after the fire of 1834. The committee was shortly superseded by a Royal Commission under the presidency of the Prince Consort. The commission determined to promote history painting (in the sense of epic narrative)

in fresco as a genre beyond the capacity of private patronage. The obvious precedent was the employment of the Nazarenes by Ludwig, Crown Prince of Bavaria at his new palace in Munich.[26]

In evidence to the Select Committee Dyce cited Bell, David Scott and himself as the only British painters possessing the necessary expertise in fresco. Evidence of this kind, although ultimately disregarded, dictated the commission's controversial policy of selecting artists by protracted public competition. In 1843 participants presented monochrome cartoons for frescoes illustrating episodes from British history or from the works of Spenser, Milton or Shakespeare. Bell's subject, derived from Holinshed's *Chronicles,* was *The Cardinal Bourchier urging the Dowager Queen of Edward IV to give up from Sanctuary the Duke of York.* His huge cartoon, measuring thirteen feet eleven inches wide by ten feet six inches high, received a second prize of £200. It survives in the form of a lithograph in the commemorative volume published by the Linnells in 1844 (fig 6). In 1844 the Commissioners invited actual specimens of fresco on a theme of the artist's choice. On this occasion Bell's entry, *Beatrice Cenci meditating the murder of her father,* was not commended. He was no more successful in the concluding competition for fresco painters to which he submitted a cartoon, a coloured sketch and a design in fresco of an allegorical figure of Justice for the House of Lords.[27]

The withholding of State patronage must have been the ultimate mortification for Bell. The temporary resuscitation during the late 1850s of an earlier prestigious commission was probably directly attributable to Bell's performance at Westminster. In 1858 he

Fig 6
BELL'S PRIZE-WINNING CARTOON, 'CARDINAL BOURCHIER'
Lithograph published 1844

showed at the Academy a 'Sketch in colour for the last arrangement of my cartoon of Richard II giving the charter to the Goldsmiths' Company' (plate 11). In 1835 and again in 1836 Bell had courted publicity for the Muirhouse and the Goldsmiths' Company schemes at the Academy. The surviving records of the Company do not mention the commission at either stage. The occasion for the first design was the opening of the new Goldsmiths' Hall in 1835. A watercolour by the architect Philip Hardwick depicting the Staircase Hall in 1839 (fig 7) proves that the project was abandoned. In 1871 the staircase was re-modelled and a later watercolour, also in the possession of the Company, appears to show one of the

staircase lunettes occupied by a narrative design in fresco. By this time Bell had reached his late seventies. The Company must also have observed the technical and aesthetic problems which beset the whole Westminster enterprise. Eventually, the Goldsmiths installed ornamental plaster grille work.[28]

While continuing to resist definition as a portraitist, Bell was still producing work of scarcely diminished quality during the 1850s. In 1852 he showed at the Royal Scottish Academy the powerful portrait of the architect David Bryce (plate 9). That year he painted, possibly as a speculation, a portrait of Michael Faraday which was still available for purchase at the Glasgow Institute in 1868. The inscription on the document in the foreground probably refers to an influential paper 'On Lines of Magnetic Force' in which Faraday expounded his theory of magneto–electricity before the Royal Society in 1851. In 1851 Faraday was honoured with membership of several European scientific academies.[29]

Recent research has revealed an equally compelling but private reason for the painting of Faraday which may offer an alternative explanation for other portrait commissions and for Bell's retention of strong links with Scotland to the very end of his career. Faraday and Bell were apparently co-

religionists. In London Faraday had long been a prominent member of the Glasite or Sandemanian church, founded by the Reverend John Glas in Dundee in 1728 as a breakaway sect of the Church of Scotland.[30] From Dundee (fig 8) the church spread to other Scottish towns and gradually into England through the vigorous proselytising of Glas's son-in-law Robert Sandeman. Biblical fundamentalists by faith and radical congregationalists in practice, the Sandemanians set themselves apart from all other Christian denominations. Among their small and scattered communities close co-operation of all kinds was essential.

Fig 7
STAIRCASE HALL, GOLDSMITHS' COMPANY
by Philip Hardwick, 1839

Fig 8
GLASITE CHAPEL OR 'KAIL KIRK',
DUNDEE
The first Glasite church, built 1777

In 1793 William Bell had been formally admitted into the Dundee community – a fact which surely influenced the choice of a rare prophetic Christian name for his second son born in 1794. John Zephaniah's mother, older brother Robert Fitzroy, sister-in-law and two nieces all became Sandemanians. From 1866 to 1874 his own name appeared annually as a visitor from London on the register of the Edinburgh meeting-house and after his death his widow Jane retained her membership of the London church.[31] Although it is uncertain where he made his own profession of faith, the accumulated evidence points to his formal membership of the London and/or the Edinburgh community.

Other pictures known to fall within this 'alternative' category include the early portrait of Charles Blair (plate 2), a Glasite at Dunkeld and comptroller or 'baron bailie' to the Duke of Atholl. By far the most impressive is the commissioned portrait of the eminent Dundee surgeon, Dr John Crichton (plate 8) which is thought to have been presented to the sitter by the Medical Faculty of the city in 1841. Crichton was a leading figure in the Dundee church for over sixty years and his daughter married one of the artist's many younger brothers.

The history of Bell's declining years is inevitably speculative. However, from the printed records of his exhibited work at the Royal Academy, the Royal Scottish Academy, the British Institution, the Royal Manchester Institution and the Glasgow Institute, a pattern emerges which is broadly consistent. His final contributions to a public exhibition were shown in Edinburgh in 1876 when he was eighty-two. During the previous decade he made a last stand as a history painter as though to assert that this was his true, if thwarted, vocation. He did so in a manner which deliberately recalled his participation in the Westminster competitions by re-utilising in large easel paintings compositions first conceived as frescoes. In 1866 he showed *Beatrice Cenci* at the Glasgow Institute with an explanatory note referring to its Westminster origins. From his London address he exhibited *Cardinal Bourchier* in Glasgow in 1865 (unsold at £210), in Manchester in 1866 at the same price and finally in Edinburgh in 1868. A second or re-worked version, dated 1870, was presented to the Tate Gallery by the artist's widow (plate 12). The same combination of vocational identity and financial necessity apparently prompted Bell's renewed involvement in art education. In 1857 and 1858 *Fraser's Magazine* published 'The Taste of the Day', three extended essays concerning style and ornament in contemporary fashion and domestic architecture in Britain. These essays represented a logical extension of Bell's work in Manchester and a belated claim for recognition as a theorist. Copy writing was also relatively lucrative. Similarly, in 1865 he offered to deliver at the Royal Scottish Academy two illustrated lectures on art (including one on history painting entitled 'Story in Art') which had already been given at the British Institution. In 1866 the lectures were presented at the Royal Manchester Institution.[32]

John Zephaniah Bell's career ended as it had begun over fifty years earlier: 'Who J. Z. Bell is we know not – oh, a Scot.' His death in South Kensington on 28 January 1883 seems to have passed unnoticed among the artistic fraternity and it was left to his co-religionists to sing his funeral elegy.

NOTES

1. *Manchester City News,* 30 September 1882, probably written by a former pupil of Bell at the Manchester School of Design and based on first-hand knowledge. The chronology is slightly confused. Bell's surviving works total eighteen, including two attributions.

2. Gerard L. Sandeman, *The Sandeman Genealogy,* Edinburgh, 1950, appendix 7: genealogy of the Bell family; Record Sederunt Book of William Bell's Sequestration 1807 to 1834 (Scottish Record Office, CS 96/4633) including biographical material.

3. S. C. Hutchison, 'The Royal Academy Schools 1768–1830' in *The Walpole Society,* vol. XXXVIII, p. 170.

4. J. Tripier le Franc, *Histoire de la Vie et de la Mort du Baron Gros,* Paris, 1880, pp. 593–608. The list of Gros's pupils (p. 583) includes both 'Ball' (?) and 'Beel', one of which may be misreading of 'Bell'

5. Airlie Muniments, Scottish Record Office, GD 16/34/387 and GD 16/34/370.

6. Keith Andrews, *The Nazarenes. A Brotherhood of German Painters in Rome,* Oxford, 1964; Allan Cunningham, *The Life of Sir David Wilkie,* London, 1843, vol. II, pp. 199, 223, 237, 277, 411; W. B. Scott, *Memoir of David Scott RSA:* entries in Scott's Roman Journal, 19 July and 9 August 1833.

7. Bell/Philips correspondence, National Library of Scotland, Acc. 10059; Royal Institution Minute-Books, Scottish Record Office, NG 3/1/1; Esmé Gordon, *The Royal Scottish Academy,* Edinburgh, 1976, pp. 44–51 and 56.

8. As shown at the Royal Society of British Artists in 1832 and reviewed in the *Gentleman's Magazine.* Bell's description of the picture – now lost – suggests an admiration for the historicism of Delaroche.

9. Airlie Muniments, Scottish Record Office, GD 16/34/387; the *Scotsman,* 3 September 1831.

10. See note 1. Bell informed Philips that the Airlie ceiling would be painted in March/April 1831.

11. In 1828 the *Edinburgh Review* published a Nazarene-inspired apologia for British patronage of fresco, even proposing Westminster Hall as a prime site (vol. XLVIII, no. XCV, pp. 61ff). In 1829 Dyce, who may have known Bell in Rome, experimented with fresco in Aberdeen (cf. Marcia Pointon, *William Dyce 1806–1864 A Critical Biography,* Oxford, 1979, p. 16).

12. *Chambers' Journal,* 17 May 1873, p. 319. The Captain was the grandfather of Randall Thomas Davidson, Archbishop of Canterbury!

13. John Small, *Castles and Mansions of the Lothians,* 1883, vol. II; *Parliamentary Papers,* vol. VI (1st Session),

1841, pp. 22–5. An analysis of the lime used by Bell was published in *The Art Union,* September 1842 (p. 209), when fresco was debated at Westminster.

14. Wilkie correspondence, National Library of Scotland, MS 9836, fo. 55; Allan Cunningham, op. cit., vol. III, p. 86; *The Times,* 28 June 1833, p. 3; *Parliamentary Papers,* vol. V, 1835, p. 375 and vol. XXI, 1836, p. 43; *Parliamentary Papers,* vol. VI (1st Session), 1841, p. 21.

15. Charles Sellers, *Oporto, Old and New,* London, 1899. In 1790 George Sandeman founded the famous firm of wine merchants based in London and Oporto. The Sandemans later inter-married with the Bells (note 2) and were co-religionists (p. 15). Any connection with Bell's Portuguese visit is speculative.

16. H. P. Livermore, *A History of Portugal,* Cambridge, 1947; Neill Macaulay, *Dom Pedro. The Struggle for Liberty in Brazil and Portugal 1798–1834,* Durham, North Carolina, 1986.

17. *The Caledonian Mercury,* 30 October 1833, and *The Glasgow Courier,* 17 October 1833; Colonel C. Shaw, *Personal Memoirs and Correspondence,* London, 1837, 2 vols, and Sir J. E. Alexander, *Sketches in Portugal during the Civil War of 1834,* London, 1835.

18. *The Glasgow Argus* and *The Glasgow Chronicle,* 30 September 1833; Post Office Annual Directory for Glasgow, 1832–5; *A Narrative of One Month's Service in the Portuguese Army in October and November 1833 by an Officer late of the Scotch Brigade,* Edinburgh, 1834.

19. Information from Alexander Waterston, Esq; E. Soares and H. de Campos Ferreira Lima, *Dicionário de Iconografia Portuguesa,* Lisbon, 1948, vol. II. The Biblioteca Nacional, Lisbon, holds an impression of this rare print.

20. Hansard Parliamentary Debates, 3rd series, vol. XLIII, 1837–8; J. S. Bell, *Journal of a Residence in Circassia during the years 1837, 1838 and 1839,* London, 1840, 2 vols; W. Ruddick (ed), J. G. Lockhart, *Peter's Letters to His Kinsfolk,* 1977, Letter XLVII.

21. See note 1 and letter from Sir William Allan, 30 November 1838, in Wilkie correspondence, National Library of Scotland, MS 9836, fo. 149. After 1831 there is no obvious evidence in the Airlie Muniments of further Airlie patronage.

22. Quentin Bell, *The Schools of Design,* London, 1963; Cecil Stewart, *A Short History of the Manchester College of Art,* n.d.

23. Autograph reminiscences of Robert Crozier (1879) and records of the Manchester School of Design (Central Library, Manchester, 707.0942 M2). See also the obituary of another Bell pupil, Warwick Brookes, in the *Manchester City News,* 26 August 1882. For Dyce's 1838 report, see *Parliamentary Papers,* vol. XXIX, 1840, pp. 25ff.

24. For Dyce's statement, see *Parliamentary Papers,* vol. XVIII, 1849, p. 65. In April 1843 Bell wrote to his friend Etty (then on the Council of the Central School) about Dyce and the Manchester affair (Etty papers, MS Y. 927, in York Library, quoted by Quentin Bell). A commentary, favouring Bell, appeared in *The Spectator,* 28 June 1845, vol. 18, pp. 618–19.

25. See Bell's statement on the Schools of Design in *The Art Union,* 1843, p. 283; *The Spectator,* 21 November 1846, p. 1122 and *The Art Union,* 1846, p. 335.

26. R. and S. Redgrave, *A Century of Painters of the English School,* London, 1866, vol. II, ch. XV; T. S. R. Boase, 'The decoration of the New Palace of Westminster 1841–1863' in *Journal of the Warburg and Courtauld Institutes,* vol. 17, 1954, pp. 319–58; David Robertson, *Sir Charles Eastlake and the Victorian Art World,* 1978.

27. On Dyce, see note 12; John, James and William Linnell, *The Prize Cartoons,* London, 1844; F. K. Hunt (ed), *The Book of Art,* London, 1846.

28. *Goldsmiths' Review,* 1988–9, p. 40. I am grateful to David Beasley for shared speculation about this project.

29. The Faraday portrait has deteriorated through successive re-painting. On Faraday, see H. Bence Jones, *The Life and Letters of Michael Faraday,* London, 1870, vol. II.

30. Geoffrey Cantor, 'Why was Faraday excluded from the Sandemanians in 1844?' in *British Journal of the History of Science,* 1989, vol. 22, pp. 433–7. Dr Cantor was the first to suggest Bell's possible religious affiliation.

31. Information from private archives extracted by Miss Joan Ferguson; Glasite church records, Dundee University Library, Archives Department, MS 9/4/1, fo. 76; see also note 2.

32. *Fraser's Magazine for Town and Country,* vol. LVI, 1857, pp. 288–96, 604–11, and vol. LVII, 1858, pp. 555–62; letter from Bell to D. O. Hill, 3 February 1865, Royal Scottish Academy; printed lecture prospectus, 22 and 29 October 1866, Manchester Central Library.

PLATES

1. Unidentified family group, *c.*1825/6.
Oil on canvas   135 × 195 cm
(Paolo Paoletti, Florence)

2. Charles Blair

Oil on canvas   76.2 × 63.5 cm

(Private collection)

3. Robert Fitzroy Bell.
Oil on canvas 91.5 × 71.2 cm
(Perth and Kinross District Council)

4. Hannah Bruce, Mrs Robert Fitzroy Bell.

Oil on canvas   76.2 × 63.5 cm

(Perth and Kinross District Council)

5. A Girl and a Soldier listening to another playing the Guitar, 1832.

Oil on canvas   71.2 × 91.5 cm

(Private collection)

6. David Ogilvy, 9th Earl of Airlie with Lady Clementina Ogilvy, 1829.

Oil on canvas   137.2 × 117.5 cm

(Private collection)

7. Maria II, Queen of Portugal, 1833.

Oil on canvas   234 × 148 cm

(Câmara Municipal, Oporto)

8. Dr John Crichton, *c*.1841.

Oil on canvas   91.5 × 71.2 cm

(Dundee Art Galleries and Museums)

9. David Bryce, 1850.

Oil on canvas   91.5 × 71.8 cm

(The Governors of the Fettes Trust)

10. Michael Faraday, 1852.

Oil on canvas   92.5 × 72.5 cm

(Hunterian Art Gallery, University of Glasgow)

11. Richard II giving the Charter to the Goldsmiths' Company, 1858.
Watercolour lunette sketch   22.8 × 63.8 cm (maximum dimensions)
(Royal Scottish Academy)

12. Cardinal Bourchier urges the widow of Edward IV to let her son out of sanctuary, 1870.

Oil on canvas   132.1 × 176.5 cm

(The Tate Gallery)

CHRONOLOGICAL CHECKLIST OF SURVIVING WORK

Further details are available from the Scottish National Portrait Gallery

1. Unidentified family group *c.*1825–6, canvas
   (Paolo Paoletti, Florence)
2. Self-portrait, canvas
   (Private collection)
3. Charles Blair, canvas
   (Private collection)
4. Anna Bell, canvas
   (Perth and Kinross District Council)
5. Hannah Bruce, Mrs R. F. Bell, canvas
   (Perth and Kinross District Council)
6. Robert Fitzroy Bell, canvas
   (Perth and Kinross District Council)
7. David Ogilvy, 9th Earl of Airlie with Lady
   Clementina Ogilvy, 1829, canvas
   (Private collection)
8. A Girl and a Soldier listening to another
   playing on a guitar, 1832, canvas
   (Private collection)
9. Ceiling at Muirhouse, 1832, fresco
   (City of Edinburgh District Council)
10. Maria II, Queen of Portugal, 1833, canvas
    (Câmara Municipal, Oporto)

11. Dr John Crichton, *c.*1841, canvas
    (Dundee Art Galleries and Museums)
12. David Bryce, 1850, canvas
    (Governors of Fettes Trust)
13. Unidentified woman, 1851, chalk drawing
    (Private collection)
14. Michael Faraday, 1852, canvas
    (Hunterian Art Gallery)
15. Richard II giving the charter to the
    Goldsmiths' Company, 1858, watercolour
    (Royal Scottish Academy)
16. Cardinal Bourchier urges the widow of
    Edward IV to let her son out of sanctuary,
    1870, canvas
    (Tate Gallery)

Works attributed to Bell

17. David Bryce, chalk drawing
    (Scottish National Portrait Gallery)
18. Professor Robert Cowan, canvas
    (Hunterian Art Gallery)

BIBLIOGRAPHY

Printed Sources

Quentin Bell, *The Schools of Design,* London 1963.

T. S. R. Boase, 'The Decoration of the New Palace
of Westminster' in *Journal of the Warburg and
Courtauld Institutes,* vol. XVII, 1954.

Edward Croft-Murray, *Decorative Painting in England
1537–1837,* vol. II, London 1970.

David and Francina Irwin, *Scottish Painters at Home
and Abroad 1700–1900,* London 1975.

Manchester City News, 26 August 1882 and 30
September 1882.

The Spectator, 21 November 1846, p. 1122.

Articles by Bell

'Schools of Design' in *The Art Union,* 1843,
p. 283.

'The Taste of the Day' in *Fraser's Magazine for Town
and Country,* vol. LVI, 1857 and vol. LVII, 1858.

Selected manuscript sources

Wilkie correspondence, National Library of
Scotland, MS 9836, fos. 55, 149; correspondence
from Bell to N. G. Philips, National Library of
Scotland, Acc. 10059; personal correspondence
(1824–31) in Airlie Muniments, Scottish Record